DOUNBY
PRIMARY SCHOOL

A CIP catalogue record for this book
is available from the British Library.

ISBN 0 7136 3312 3

First published by A & C Black (Publishers) Limited,
35 Bedford Row, London WC1R 4JH

Acknowledgements

The illustrations are by Jakki Wood

Photographs by Jenny Mathews, except for p8–9, 18, Chris
Fairclough, p11(t), p12 ROSPA, p16, Richard and Sally
Greenhill, p22 London Borough of Hackney Planning
Department, p22 (inset) Ecoscene, p23 GEC Traffic
Automation Limited. Back cover, Chris Fairclough.

The authors and publisher would like to thank the following
people whose help and co-operation made this book
possible: the staff and pupils of Bounds Green Junior school.

Typeset by August Filmsetting, Haydock, St Helens
Printed in Belgium by Proost International Book Production

Roads

KATE PETTY and TERRY CASH

Photographs by Jenny Matthews

Contents

TRACKS

A&C Black · London

All sorts of roads

What sort of road do you live in?

Is it a road which is hardly more than a pathway or an alley? Or a narrow lane, winding through the countryside?

Maybe you live on a busy high street with shops and offices, where buses and lorries rumble past your window. Not many people live right by a motorway.

You probably travel on roads every day to get from one place to another. How do you get to school?

If you come by car or bus, the driver has to follow the road along one-way streets across junctions and around roundabouts.

If you walk, you might know shortcuts down alleys and side streets. Maybe you have to cross a busy road.

How would your journey be different if the roads were blocked – by snow, for instance?

Routes and maps

You can draw a picture of your journey to school. It will be a map of the roads you use. Make a rough drawing first so that it fits on the page. You should include your home, the school, and landmarks such as a church, a park, a factory or a shopping parade. Put in the street names as well.

Now compare your picture map with a road map of the area. Did you leave anything out? Is it the same way up (most maps will show north at the top)? Do your long roads look longer than your short roads?

See who takes the longest route to school. You will need a large-scale map of the area and some lengths of different-coloured wool.

Stick one pin where your home is and another in the school. Now put a pin at each place where you turn a corner on your journey. Wind the wool round the pins to show your journey to school. Now get your friends to trace their routes to school.

Take the pieces of wool off the maps and compare the lengths. Who has the longest journey? Can you find a quicker way of going from your home to school? Now use the wool to mark a straight line between your home and your school. Why can't you travel this route? What gets in the way?

Roads long ago

People and animals have always made tracks and trails from one place to another. Gradually the quickest or safest route gets worn into a path.

Have you ever made a path by taking the same short cut lots of times? It's fine in dry weather, but in wet weather, paths soon become muddy places that bog you down. If lots of people take the same path it becomes unusable.

Over 2000 years ago the Romans worked out a way of solving this problem and became expert road builders. They needed roads so that they could transport their armies, with all their horses and wagons, along the shortest route from one place to another. Good roads also meant that messengers could carry news quickly and keep their rulers up to date with what was happening in other towns.

The Romans knew that for a road to be passable all year round it needs some sort of hard surface, and it needs to be well drained. First the Roman road builders made layers of chalk and stones which would allow water to drain away. They built the surface higher in the middle than at the edges so that water would run off into deep ditches dug on either side of the road. They laid paving stones or cobbles on top to make a hard surface.

stone slabs
gravel
rammed chalk
gravel
rammed chalk
flints

Roman roads were built in as straight a line as possible between two places. Some of our straightest roads still follow old Roman routes. See if there is one near where you live.

Building a road today

Road engineers today have to deal with many of the same problems as the Roman road builders: a modern road should be a convenient route between one place and another, it should have a surface strong enough to take the weight of traffic, and should be well drained.

The route of a new road is planned using aerial photographs and maps. The surveyor uses a special instrument called a theodolite to find a route that will be as level as possible.

After the engineers have worked out what sort of ground the road will be built on, trenches for drainage are dug. Why do you think this is done so early on?

Now the huge earth-moving machines can begin to roll. Excavators and bulldozers clear a path. Then grading machines level the ground off.

The earth forms the bottom layer of the new road. It is packed down firmly. The next layer is made up of crushed stones and gravel. Some roads are then given a layer of concrete. The upper layer is laid by a machine called a paver. It is made from a hot sticky mixture of tar and small stones, and is called macadam.

Now the road is ready for the final 'wearing surface' which cars will drive on.

Road surfaces

The surface of a road has to be very strong to carry traffic. It mustn't crack in extreme heat or cold, and it needs to be smooth so that passengers don't have a bumpy ride.

Several different materials are used for surfacing roads. Have you ever travelled over cobbles, or bricks, or gravel? Most roads are covered with asphalt or concrete.

Asphalt is made of crushed stones and sand, held together by sticky black bitumen. Layers of the hot treacly asphalt are spread on the new road and rolled until they are smooth.

A concrete surface feels much harder than an asphalt one. When a concrete surface is laid, steel netting is sandwiched between layers of wet concrete to strengthen it when it sets.

A slippery road surface can be very dangerous for drivers. Tyres cannot grip and the car can start to slide and skid. Tyres are made with a pattern called a tread, which helps them to grip better, but even these will not always work on a very smooth surface, like ice.

When the road is icy, people put salt and grit on the roads. Try putting salt on some ice? What happens? Why do you think grit is added to the salt?

Rain water can make a road slippery, too, but good road drainage and good tyres should stop a car skidding.

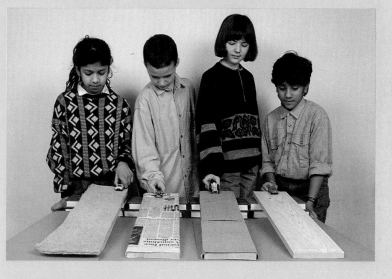

Which surface is the fastest?

You will need

some toy cars

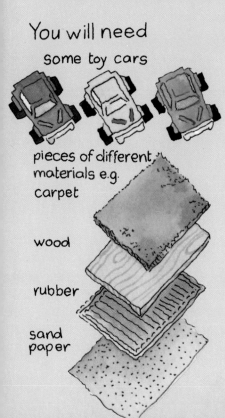

pieces of different materials e.g. carpet

wood

rubber

sand paper

Guess which surface your cars will run on fastest. Then try each material to see if you are right.

Finding the way

Before a new road is opened to the public, it needs road markings, signs and petrol stations, and perhaps crash barriers and street lights too – to make driving easier and safer.

White lines on the road show drivers where they can go, whether they can overtake, and where to stop.

Sign posts give directions, warn of dangers ahead, and give orders to the driver.

Look at these signs.

Which shape shows the sign is a warning?
Which shape shows that the sign is an order?

Signs on main roads and motorways are big and well lit so that a driver can read them at speed. These signs give distances and directions.

Signs on main roads have a green background. Other signs have different colour backgrounds. Why do you think they are coloured like this? Experiment with different colours. Which two colours can be seen best from a distance? Which colours aren't so bright?

Road signs are very useful, but a longer journey is easier if you plan it first with a map. Here are some of the things you might see on a journey, with the map symbols beside them.

Road safety

A road is a dangerous place, even if it is well looked after, and motorists follow the road signs carefully. Every year over three hundred school children are killed on the roads in Britain. Thirty five thousand are injured and need to go to hospital.

Learn to cross the road safely:

Children under eight years old should try always to cross the road with an adult.

You should use a footbridge or subway if there is one. If not, the safest places are where there is a school crossing patrol or a pedestrian crossing. Traffic lights and traffic islands can also make crossing safer.

The Green Cross Code tells you what to do every time you cross a road where there aren't any of these things:

Find a place where you can see the road clearly, then stop.

Wait on the pavement near the kerb.

Look all around for traffic and listen.

If traffic is coming, wait for it to pass. Look all around again.

When there is no traffic near, walk straight across the road.

Keep looking and listening for traffic while you cross.

See and be seen

When the light is poor, you are almost invisible to a driver. Look at the coats these children are wearing. Which one is the easiest to see?

Pale clothes and fluorescent colours show up best in the dark. You can also wear reflective bands, which shine in the lights of a car.

Traffic lights

If there were no traffic lights, traffic at a busy road junction would soon grind to a halt. Traffic lights keep the traffic moving and make sure that drivers wait their turn at junctions.

Every set of traffic lights has a control box nearby. This is the computer which gives information to the traffic lights about how many people are waiting, and how busy the traffic is.

In many towns, there is a big central computer which is connected to all the small control boxes. An engineer can use the big computer to work out the best way to keep traffic moving through the town.

Make a working set of miniature traffic lights

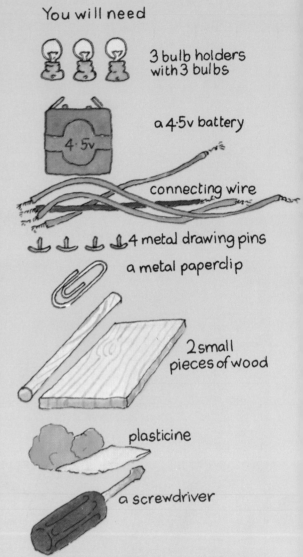

You will need

3 bulb holders with 3 bulbs

a 4.5v battery

connecting wire

4 metal drawing pins

a metal paperclip

2 small pieces of wood

plasticine

a screwdriver

1. Attach the bulbs in a row to one of the pieces of wood, using glue or sellotape. Stand the piece of wood in some plasticine.

2. Stick the drawing pins in the other piece of wood, in the pattern shown in diagram (a).

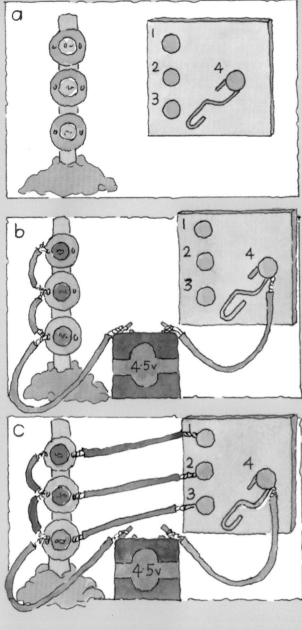

3. Fit the paper clip round drawing pin number 4.

4. Use the wire to attach one side of the bulb holder to the next. Attach the wire from the bottom bulb to one terminal on the battery.

5. Attach another wire from the other battery terminal to drawing pin number 4. See diagram (b).

6. Cover each bulb with cellophane matching each colour of the traffic lights. You can use sellotape to hold the cellophane on.

7. Use the wire to connect the red light to drawing pin 1, the amber light to drawing pin 2, and the green light to drawing pin 3. See diagram (c).

Now your traffic lights are ready to use. If you touch the drawing pins with the paper clip, you should be able to make them shine in sequence. Touch number 1 & 2 together to make the red and amber lights come on together.

Keeping the traffic moving

Every year, more people in this country use a car to travel. Many British roads weren't designed to cope with so much traffic. If there is an accident, or the road needs repairing or there are just too many cars on a narrow stretch of road – you get a traffic jam.

On a motorway, a contra-flow system is sometimes used to keep traffic moving when part of the road is being repaired. Traffic cones direct traffic into another lane, sometimes on the opposite side of the motorway.

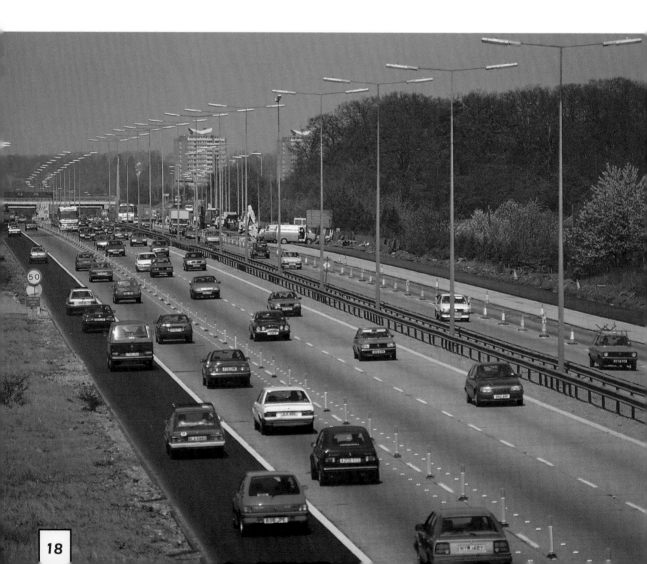

Every day thousands of cars have to pass through the streets of towns that were laid out long before the car was invented. Different towns deal with the traffic in different ways.

Some towns have a bypass, where a new road is built to take the traffic round the outskirts of the town. In a one-way system all the cars have to follow the same route round the town centre. Some towns have a park and ride, where shoppers can leave their cars on the edge of town and use a free bus to travel to the centre of town.

◀ In a pedestrian precinct, some streets are cut off to traffic and set aside just for pedestrians.

Bus lanes and bicycle ▶ lanes make it faster to use public transport or ride a bike.

Roads and our environment

Over half a kilogramme of poisonous waste pours out of an average car every day. The waste gases produced by the engine contain lead, which can cause brain damage in growing children, carbon monoxide, which can affect the heart, nitrous oxide, which causes acid rain, and carbon dioxide, which adds to the 'greenhouse effect', warming up the atmosphere.

Recently, many people have started to use unleaded petrol, and soon new cars will have to be fitted with catalytic converters, which help to remove most of the poisons before they come out of the exhaust pipe.

Some scientists are experimenting with other sorts of fuel or electricity to power the cars of the future.

Wildlife near roads

Lots of different kinds of wildlife live in the hedgerows along country lanes. Look out for toads or rabbits or hedgehogs. You probably won't see many wild animals near a motorway. Many of them only come out at night – you can see their eyes reflected in the car lights. Motorway verges are not disturbed by people so lots of different wild flowers grow on them.

Look out for different kinds of birds, too. You may be able to see a kestrel hovering high above the road, searching for its prey. There are often crows by the side of the road, too.

Look out for road signs which tell you there are deer, toads or ducks nearby.

Into the twenty-first century

Is building more roads the best way to keep traffic moving?
As our roads get more and more blocked, new roads are
being planned. Town planners have to work out the best
route, taking into consideration parks, houses and schools.

Can you see the proposed motorway-link road marked in
yellow and outlined in black on the right of this picture? Why
do you think local people might not want it?

Some of the newest cars are fitted with computers which warn the driver if the car is not working properly. Some of these computers can even speak. A car computer is being tested which can work out the best route for the driver to take, avoiding any traffic jams.

Eventually cars could become completely computer controlled, so the driver could just sit back and watch a video. Or the road could move like a conveyor belt, instead of the cars.

But are cars the best way of travelling? A car often carries only one passenger into a town at rush hour. This means forty cars clog the road, carrying drivers who could all be carried in just one bus.

Perhaps cars will be banned from big cities, which will then be turned into huge pedestrian precincts with bus lanes.

What do you think will happen to traffic in the future?

Facts

The **oldest** known 'road' in Britain, the Sweet Way in Somerset, is roughly **24,000 years old**. Parts of roads built by the Romans in Britain 2,000 years ago still exist: Watling Street (346 km) ran from Dover to Wroxeter; the Fosse Way (350 km) went from Lincoln to Exeter.

The Pan American Highway is the **longest** road in the world. It stretches all the way from the top to the bottom of the Americas – from Alaska to Chile – and then eastwards to Brasilia, Brazil.

Also in Brasilia is the **widest** road in the world, the Monumental Axis, which is **250 m** across although it has only six lanes. The toll plaza before Oakland Bridge in California is 23 lanes wide. At Linnyshaw Moss, near Manchester, the M61 motorway is 17 lanes wide.

Italy claims the **narrowest** street. Vicolo del Virilita in the village of Ripatransone is **43 cm** wide.

The East Los Angeles Interchange in California, USA, has the **highest volume** of traffic in the world. **Every minute 363 vehicles** pass through.

'Spaghetti Junction' is the name usually given to the the most complex interchange in Britain – on the M6 motorway, just north of Birmingham. There are **18 routes on 6 different levels**.

The Avius Autobahn was the first of Germany's Autobahn network to be opened, in 1921. The **first motorway** was opened in Italy in **1924**. The first British motorway, the M6 Preston Bypass, was opened in 1958.

Early traffic lights
The United States had the first traffic lights in 1919 in Detroit. They were first introduced in Britain in 1928, although it wasn't until two years later, in 1930, that it became an offence to disobey them!

Going green
Poisonous gases in a car's exhaust pollute the air and contribute towards global warming. Yet most of us travel in cars for short and often unnecessary journeys. One-third of all journeys are under one mile; one-half are under two miles. Start walking to school and to other places near by! You will be fitter and there will be fewer cars on the roads.